Threads of
Poems for t

While every precaution has been taken in the preparation of this book, the publisher assumes no responsibility for errors or omissions, or for damages resulting from the use of the information contained herein.

THREADS OF EXISTENCE POEMS FOR THE SOUL.

First edition. November 20, 2024.

Copyright © 2024 Darryl De Carteret Pochin.

ISBN: 979-8230306719

Written by Darryl De Carteret Pochin.

Threads of Existence
Poems for the Soul.

By
Darryl De Carteret Pochin

Prologue

In the quiet moments of life, when the rush subsides and the world feels still, poetry emerges as a voice for the heart. These poems are reflections of the human journey, woven from the threads of our shared experiences and the emotions that bind us. They explore the many facets of existence, from the profound to the everyday, capturing the essence of what it means to live, love, and grow.

The poems delve into **Life**, with its twists and turns, its trials and triumphs, reminding us of the beauty found in every fleeting moment. They celebrate **Friendship**, the bonds that anchor us in love and laughter, and they honour **Family**, the roots from which we draw our strength. In the verses about **Love**, we touch the infinite, its passion, its depth, and its quiet constancy.

In the garden, a place of peace and renewal, we find metaphors for growth, patience, and hope. In the poems about **God**, we explore faith, grace, and the divine presence that guides us through life's challenges. Finally, the verses on **Work** reflect the dignity of effort, the satisfaction of creation, and the purpose found in the toil of our hands.

Each poem is a meditation, an invitation to pause and reflect, to find meaning in the ordinary and extraordinary alike. Together, they form a tapestry, a celebration of the human spirit and its enduring search for connection, purpose, and joy.

Poems About Life

The Journey

Life is a road, winding and vast,
A present moment, tied to the past.
Each step we take, a story unfolds,
Of dreams we chase, of courage we hold.
Some paths are smooth, others are steep,
Each turn we take, a memory we keep.
The sun may shine, the storms may roar,
But we move forward, seeking more.
Through every trial, joy, or pain,
We find the strength to try again.

Seasons of Life

Life moves like seasons, one by one,
A circle turning beneath the sun.
Spring awakens with seeds of green,
In summer's fire, we dare to dream.
Autumn whispers of changes near,
Winter holds us in moments clear.
Each has a purpose, a time, a place,
To slow us down or quicken our pace.
In every season, growth is found,
Through joy or loss, the world spins round.

A Moment's Breath

Pause for a moment and just be still,
Feel the air, the space you fill.
The world spins on, it never waits,
Yet in your hands, you hold your fate.
Life is fleeting, a candle's flame,
It burns for love, not wealth or fame.
Each breath you take is a chance to see,
The beauty of life's mystery.
So slow your steps, release your fears,
And find the magic in your years.

The Canvas

Life is a canvas, blank and bare,
With strokes of love and hues of care.
The colours run, some blend, some stain,
Through joy and sorrow, through loss and gain.
Mistakes may linger, dark and wide,
Yet beauty's born where shadows collide.
Each brushstroke tells a tale unique,
Of moments loud and moments meek.
No masterpiece is ever planned,
Create your art with heart in hand.

The Dance

Life is a dance, a rhythm divine,
A waltz of moments, yours and mine.
The music plays, some slow, some fast,
We sway to the tune of the present and past.
At times, our feet may stumble and fall,
Yet we rise again, giving it our all.
In every step, we learn, we grow,
The beauty of life begins to show.
Through laughter, tears, and every chance,
We find ourselves within the dance.

Whispers of Time

Time moves softly, like wind through the trees,
Carrying moments on gentle breeze.
It does not shout, nor does it stay,
But whispers, urging us on our way.
Each tick of the clock, a gift, a choice,
A fleeting second, a silenced voice.
Do not let it slip through your grasp,
Hold it tight in every task.
For time is a treasure, precious and rare,
Use it wisely, with love and care.

Mountains and Valleys

Life is a journey of peaks and lows,
Through rugged trails and soft meadows.
The mountains call with a challenge steep,
The valleys cradle where shadows creep.
But neither space defines the soul,
It's in the climb we find our goal.
Each step forward, a story made,
With strength found in light and shade.
For every summit, we must prepare,
Life's beauty lives in the journey there.

Life's Thread

Life is a thread, fine and thin,
A woven tale where we begin.
Each stitch we make, each strand we tie,
Builds a tapestry beneath the sky.
Silver for wisdom, gold for cheer,
Shades of grey for every tear.
Threads may fray, but still they mend,
A fabric strong until the end.
Life's pattern grows with every seam,
A quilt of love, a cherished dream.

The Mirror

Life's a mirror, reflecting true,
It gives us back what we pursue.
Smile, and kindness will appear,
Frown, and shadows linger near.
The world's a glass, polished and bright,
Shaped by our choices, dark or light.
If you give love, it multiplies,
If you share joy, the spirit flies.
See yourself in what you give,
For that's the way we truly live.

Unwritten

Life is a book with pages bare,
An open story, waiting there.
The pen is yours, the ink your soul,
The words you write make you whole.
Some chapters end, some dreams are new,
Some lines are false, others true.
Write with courage, love, and grace,
Let every page leave its trace.
For when the story is said and done,
Your life's a tale for everyone.

Poems About Friendship

The Ties That Bind

Friendship is a thread, strong and fine,
Weaving lives, yours and mine.
Through laughter shared and tears we shed,
A bond grows deeper with words unsaid.
It isn't measured by time or space,
But by the love that leaves its trace.
When the world feels heavy, dark, and cold,
A friend's warm touch is purest gold.
So cherish the ties, fragile yet strong,
For they hold us close, where we belong.

A Friend's Embrace

In the quiet storms of life's long race,
There's solace found in a friend's embrace.
Not just in joy, but in times of despair,
They stand beside you, always there.
A friend's smile can heal the soul,
Their kindness mends, their laughter whole.
No burden too heavy, no task too small,
With a true friend, you conquer all.
Through every triumph, loss, or start,
A friend's love stays, a work of art.

Kindred Souls

Friendship blooms in the strangest of places,
Among strangers with different faces.
A shared laugh, a knowing glance,
A bond is forged by chance.
Kindred souls, though far or near,
Find connection in love sincere.
No barriers of time or tongue,
Just hearts where shared songs are sung.
With every word, the bond extends,
For life is richer with true friends.

Unseen Threads

Friendship's threads are soft yet strong,
Invisible ties where hearts belong.
They hold us steady, pull us near,
Through every joy and every tear.
Though time may stretch or distance grow,
The ties remain, as we both know.
A friend's voice echoes in the mind,
With comfort rare and love refined.
Unseen, unbroken, forever true,
Friendship is life's greatest glue.

The Gift of Friendship

A friend is a gift, no ribbon required,
A presence that leaves you forever inspired.
They know your fears, your silent cries,
And lift your spirit to brighter skies.
Their laughter fills the empty air,
A soothing balm when life's unfair.
Through storms and sun, they stay the same,
A light to guide, a gentle flame.
In their embrace, you find your place,
A haven of warmth, a sacred space.

A Circle of Friends

Friendship forms a circle wide,
A bond of love, where hearts reside.
Each hand we hold, each name we share,
Builds a haven beyond compare.
It's not the length of time that shows,
But the joy that in each moment grows.
Through years or seconds, it stays alive,
A spark that helps the soul survive.
In a friend's embrace, no fear can stay,
For love will always light the way.

The Bridge

Friendship is a bridge we cross,
Spanning gaps of time or loss.
Its sturdy planks, though worn and old,
Carry weight that's rich with gold.
No river wide, no canyon deep,
Can keep us from the vows we keep.
When life's storms threaten the view,
A friend will always see you through.
Each step upon this bridge we take,
Is trust and love we'll never forsake.

Forever and Always

A true friend's love is evergreen,
A constant light in shadows unseen.
Through every chapter, old or new,
They stand beside, loyal and true.
No need for words, they understand,
The language spoken heart to hand.
And even when the roads divide,
You'll find them there, by your side.
Forever's not just a word we say,
It's a promise lived, day by day.

Laughter and Tears

A friend is there for laughter bright,
And stays through tears in the darkest night.
They see the cracks and love you still,
A bond that neither time nor pain can kill.
In their presence, the world feels whole,
A sanctuary for the soul.
They hold your fears, they cheer your dreams,
Through all life's unexpected streams.
A friend is not just someone near,
But the one who makes your path clear.

Friendship's Flame

Friendship burns like a steady flame,
Unfazed by wind, untouched by blame.
Its glow is soft, yet warm and true,
A light that brightens all you do.
Though days may darken, shadows grow,
The flame persists, a constant glow.
It doesn't falter, it doesn't fade,
Through storms and trials, it's unafraid.
In friendship's light, we find our way,
A beacon that forever stays.

Poems About Family

Roots and Branches
Family stands like a tree so strong,
Roots run deep, where we belong.
The trunk holds firm through storm and strife,
A sheltering force, the heart of life.
Branches stretch to touch the skies,
Reaching upward as time flies.
Leaves may fall, but seasons bring,
New growth, renewal, eternal spring.
Though winds may whisper or tempests call,
Family endures, it weathers all.

A Circle of Love

A family's love is a boundless ring,
A place where hearts learn how to sing.
Through every fight and every tear,
It's family's love that keeps us near.
A mother's touch, a father's care,
A sibling's laughter fills the air.
Though distance comes or years unfold,
The circle remains, its bond pure gold.
No matter where our lives may roam,
Family's love will bring us home.

The First Home

Family is the first embrace,
The origin of love's warm grace.
A mother's lullaby, soft and low,
A father's wisdom helping us grow.
Siblings teach us how to share,
Laughter echoes everywhere.
It's where we learn, it's where we fall,
It's where we're loved through it all.
Through life's twists, it stays the same,
The first to cheer, the first to name.

Family Ties

Invisible strings connect us all,
From joyous heights to shadows' fall.
Through every triumph, every scar,
Family knows just who we are.
They see our flaws, they know our fears,
But stand beside us through the years.
These ties can stretch, but never break,
Through all we give and all we take.
For family's love, though tested, true,
Is the strength that carries you.

A Mother's Love

A mother's love is boundless and wide,
A gentle hand, a constant guide.
It heals the wounds we cannot see,
And whispers, "You're enough for me."
Her voice is soft, yet firm and strong,
A steady rhythm, life's first song.
She sees the good when the world turns cold,
A quiet hero, brave and bold.
Through every moment, dark or bright,
A mother's love is endless light.

A Father's Strength

A father's strength is steady and sure,
A quiet love that will endure.
His hands are rough, his words may be few,
But his heart beats fiercely for you.
He stands as a shield when storms appear,
A steadfast presence, calm and clear.
In every lesson, in every deed,
He plants the seeds we'll always need.
A father's love, though hard to see,
Is a fortress built for family.

Siblings' Song

Siblings are the songs we share,
The playful notes that fill the air.
Through teasing words and petty fights,
They hold us close on darkest nights.
A shared childhood, memories vast,
Stories written that always last.
They know your secrets, your hopes, your fears,
And laugh with you through the years.
Though paths may part, their love remains,
A constant melody through joys and pains.

Generations

Generations pass, yet still they weave,
A story told, a legacy to leave.
Grandparents' hands, soft and wise,
Their lives etched in time's deep skies.
Parents nurture with love so pure,
Their sacrifices will always endure.
Children grow, yet the roots stay true,
The past lives on in what they do.
A family's strength is its endless chain,
A bond that time cannot restrain.

Coming Home

Home is not a place or land,
But where your family takes your hand.
It's in the hugs, the knowing smiles,
The stories shared across the miles.
The smell of meals that stir the heart,
The feeling of never being apart.
No matter how far your journey leads,
It's family's love that fills your needs.
Coming home is more than a door,
It's finding where love lives evermore.

The Heart of Family

Family is the heart of life,
A steady force through joy and strife.
It teaches patience, love, and care,
A bond that grows beyond compare.
Through whispered prayers and endless fights,
It holds us close on sleepless nights.
It isn't perfect, it's messy, flawed,
But through it all, we remain awed.
For family is where life begins,
A sacred bond that always wins.

Poems About Love

<u>The Language of Love</u>

Love speaks softly, in quiet tones,
In gentle whispers when you're alone.
It's in the glance, the fleeting smile,
The steady hand that stays a while.
It knows no borders, no space, no time,
A language pure, both yours and mine.
It lifts the weary, it heals the heart,
A force unbroken, a sacred art.
For love is endless, boundless, free,
A bridge between you and me.

Love's Light

Love is a light, warm and pure,
A flame that flickers but will endure.
It shines through storms, it calms the seas,
It whispers hope on the softest breeze.
Though shadows try to dim its glow,
Love's radiant strength will always show.
It guides the lost, it soothes the weak,
In every soul, it dares to speak.
No matter the distance, the trials, the night,
Love remains, our guiding light.

The Rhythm of Love

Love moves like music, a rhythm divine,
A melody sweet, a perfect line.
Its tempo shifts, from slow to fast,
Yet every note is meant to last.
It dances in hearts, it soars in skies,
It's found in laughter, in teary eyes.
Love is the song we sing each day,
A timeless tune that won't decay.
Through every verse, each fleeting phrase,
Love is the music that always stays.

Love's Garden

Love is a garden, lush and wide,
Where seeds of kindness bloom with pride.
Each flower grows through tender care,
Its roots entwined beyond compare.
Though storms may come, the petals sway,
Love finds its strength in every way.
It thrives in hearts, it never fades,
Through darkest nights and brightest days.
With every touch, each gentle rain,
Love blossoms again and again.

Boundless Love

Love knows no walls, no chains, no ties,
It reaches where the heart still cries.
It soars beyond the tallest spire,
A burning force, an endless fire.
No borders hold it, no time contains,
It flows through loss, through joys, through pains.
It's in the hug, the touch, the tear,
The quiet presence that draws you near.
Boundless, fearless, wild, and free,
Love is all we're meant to be.

A Love Eternal

Time may wither, the world may change,
Yet love endures, vast and strange.
It does not falter, it does not fade,
It holds the promises we've made.
Through every season, it stays the same,
A flickering fire, a steady flame.
When all is gone, when skies turn grey,
Love will guide us, show the way.
Its echoes linger, soft and sweet,
A bond unbroken, complete.

The Gift of Love

Love is a gift, unwrapped, unbound,
A treasure rare, where joy is found.
It asks for nothing, yet gives its all,
It catches you when you start to fall.
Its value grows with every year,
A soothing balm for every tear.
It's in the small, the grand, the unseen,
The moments in life that lie between.
No price can buy it, no force can take,
For love is the gift we always make.

First Love

First love blooms like spring's first kiss,
A fleeting taste of life's sweet bliss.
Its petals open, soft and new,
A world transformed, a brighter hue.
Each heartbeat quickens, each glance divine,
The world stands still, and you are mine.
Though seasons change and time moves on,
The echo of first love is never gone.
A memory pure, a sacred place,
Where love's first light forever stays.

Love's Strength

Love is stronger than fear or hate,
It bends but breaks not beneath its weight.
It fights for peace, it shields the weak,
It stands for all that we seek.
Its strength is quiet, a gentle touch,
It heals the wounds we feel too much.
It holds the world with steady hands,
A power no force can withstand.
In love, we find the strength to rise,
And see the world through hopeful eyes.

A Love to Last

Some love is fleeting, some burns fast,
But true love's flame is built to last.
It weathers storms, it passes tests,
It settles deep within our chests.
It's in the trust, the words unspoken,
The promises that stay unbroken.
It doesn't waver, it doesn't stray,
It grows with time, come what may.
A love to last is rare and true,
A bond eternal, between me and you.

Poems About Your Garden

The Gardener's Touch

A garden blooms beneath your care,
Each seed a promise planted there.
Your hands, with soil, gentle and wise,
Coax life from earth beneath the skies.
The sun's warm glow, the rain's embrace,
Bring forth a world of endless grace.
Petals soft, their colours bright,
Awaken the day, embrace the night.
Each leaf, each stem, a story told,
Of nature's gifts, both green and gold.

Morning in the Garden

In morning light, the garden wakes,
With dewdrops clinging to the stakes.
The roses blush, the daisies sway,
Welcoming the brand-new day.
A sparrow sings, a breeze hums low,
Through leafy arches, shadows grow.
Here time slows down, its rush erased,
In this quiet, sacred, peaceful space.
The garden breathes, alive and free,
A world of wonder, just for me.

The Symphony of Growth

The garden hums a quiet tune,
From dawn's first light to the rise of the moon.
The rustle of leaves, the buzzing of bees,
The whisper of wind through towering trees.
Each flower's bloom a melody sweet,
Each root a rhythm beneath your feet.
Together they play, this song of the earth,
A hymn to life, renewal, and birth.
In this symphony, hearts find rest,
For nature's music is always best.

Seasons of the Garden

Spring breathes life, with colours bright,
Soft petals bathed in morning light.
Summer thrives with heat and rain,
A bounty grows in every vein.
Autumn paints the garden gold,
Leaves fall, their stories bold.
Winter hushes, the earth takes rest,
Beneath its blanket, nature's best.
The garden flows with seasons' art,
A living rhythm, a beating heart.

The Secret Garden

Within the gate, a world concealed,
Where nature's wonders are revealed.
The lilacs bloom, their fragrance sweet,
The grass is soft beneath your feet.
A butterfly drifts through the air,
Its colours bright, beyond compare.
The ivy climbs the garden wall,
A peaceful haven, after all.
This secret space, a sacred part,
A quiet refuge for the heart.

The Gardener's Wisdom

The garden teaches, year by year,
That patience blooms when skies aren't clear.
A single seed holds endless worth,
A testament to life's rebirth.
The weeds may come, the pests invade,
But love endures where roots are laid.
Through trial and care, a harvest grows,
The gardener reaps the joy he sows.
In every sprout, a lesson lives:
Life rewards the heart that gives.

The Colours of the Garden

The garden bursts with a painter's hand,
Colours woven, bright and grand.
The crimson rose, the daisy's white,
The golden sunflowers reaching height.
Green leaves frame this masterpiece,
A living canvas, a moment's peace.
The palette shifts as seasons flow,
From summer's heat to winter's snow.
In every shade, in every hue,
The garden sings a song anew.

The Heart of the Earth

The garden's soil, dark and deep,
Holds secrets nature longs to keep.
Its fertile heart, where roots descend,
Becomes the place where life begins.
The worms, the stones, the ancient clay,
All play a part in life's ballet.
Each spade of earth, each seed you sow,
Becomes the magic of what will grow.
From earth's warm heart, the garden springs,
A quiet space where nature sings.

The Butterfly's Realm

The garden is a butterfly's throne,
A kingdom vast, yet softly grown.
They flutter by on painted wings,
Touching flowers, life's tiny kings.
Each bloom they kiss, a fleeting grace,
Transforming time, slowing its pace.
Their beauty speaks in whispers rare,
A fleeting wonder beyond compare.
Within this space, so calm, so bright,
The butterflies dance in nature's light.

Eternal Bloom

The garden blooms, then fades away,
Yet beauty returns another day.
The roses rest, the tulips sleep,
The seasons promise what they keep.
For life renews in endless streams,
A gardener's hope, a planter's dream.
No end can claim this sacred space,
Where life and love leave their trace.
The garden blooms, eternal, pure,
Through death, rebirth will always endure.

Poems About God

God's Presence

In quiet moments, soft and still,
We feel the whisper of God's will.
A guiding hand, a calming voice,
A love that leaves us with no choice.
To trust, to hope, to rise each day,
And walk the path He lights our way.
Through trials hard and blessings sweet,
In every heartbeat, His love we meet.
For God is near, in joy, in pain,
A steady presence we can't explain.

The Creator's Hand

Look to the sky, the earth, the seas,
Each crafted with divine expertise.
The stars that glitter, the rivers that flow,
The hand of God is all we know.
In every leaf, in every grain,
His artistry will ever remain.
The mountains rise, the valleys fall,
His power and grace encompass all.
A masterpiece no man could plan,
The universe holds the Creator's hand.

A Prayer

Lord, hear my prayer, soft and true,
I offer my heart, my soul to You.
In joy, I thank, in pain, I plea,
Guide my steps, stay close to me.
Your mercy shines, Your love profound,
In You, my strength and hope are found.
Through every storm, You lead the way,
Your light turns night into day.
Forever grateful, I shall be,
For Your endless love has set me free.

God's Love

God's love is vast, no bounds contain,
A grace that soothes the deepest pain.
It heals the broken, lifts the weak,
A love that every soul can seek.
It shines in moments grand and small,
In silent prayers or a sparrow's call.
No force on earth could break this bond,
It's infinite, timeless, and far beyond.
God's love is all, it's in the air,
A gift eternal, beyond compare.

The Shepherd

God is the shepherd, gentle and kind,
Seeking the lost, no sheep left behind.
Through darkest valleys, He leads the way,
His voice a guide, His love our stay.
The pastures green, the waters still,
All flow beneath His perfect will.
Though paths may twist, though shadows fall,
The Shepherd guards and saves us all.
In His embrace, we're safe, secure,
His love and grace forever endure.

The Light of God

God's light shines bright, a beacon clear,
Dispelling darkness, drawing near.
It warms the soul, it clears the mind,
It leaves no fear or doubt behind.
A fire that burns through endless night,
A guide for those who seek the right.
Its radiance shows the path we tread,
Where every tear and pain is shed.
In God's great light, we find our way,
To peace eternal, come what may.

God's Timing

God's time is perfect, never late,
A plan unfolds, designed by fate.
Though we may question, plead, or doubt,
His wisdom knows what life's about.
Each moment's placed with love and care,
Each trial a gift, a secret prayer.
For in the waiting, hearts will grow,
A deeper faith, His grace to show.
Trust in His timing, firm and true,
For God is always guiding you.

God's Promise

God promises a love divine,
A covenant that stands through time.
He'll never leave, He'll never stray,
Through every night and endless day.
His mercy flows like streams of gold,
A truth that never will grow old.
He promised joy beyond this life,
An end to sorrow, pain, and strife.
God's promise stands, a beacon bright,
A hope that guides us through the night.

God in the Small Things

God's in the small things, soft and still,
In the blooming flower, the whippoorwill.
In a child's laugh, in a stranger's smile,
In every inch, in every mile.
He's in the rain that cools the air,
In every answered, quiet prayer.
He's in the bread, the wine, the light,
In darkest hours and morning bright.
Look closely, see His gentle care,
For God's great love is everywhere.

Eternal Grace

God's grace flows like an endless stream,
A gift beyond our wildest dream.
It lifts the fallen, it breaks the chain,
It soothes the soul through every pain.
Undeserved, yet freely given,
A glimpse of heaven, a taste of the forgiven.
No sin too great, no heart too cold,
His grace renews, it makes us bold.
Eternal, boundless, and divine,
Through God's great grace, we truly shine.

Poems About Work

The Labourers Song
Work is a rhythm, steady and true,
Each task a verse, each day anew.
From sunrise glow to twilight's rest,
We give our all, we do our best.
The hands may tire, the back may ache,
But purpose burns in what we make.
Through sweat and toil, dreams are built,
A legacy free of shame or guilt.
The labourer's song is one of pride,
A melody where strength resides.

The Fruits of Work

Work is a seed we plant with care,
Its fruits a harvest beyond compare.
Each effort sown, each hour spent,
Brings growth and joy, our lives' intent.
Through struggles fierce and trials long,
Our spirit grows steadfast and strong.
No task too small, no effort vain,
For work brings lessons, peace, and gain.
Reap the rewards, both near and far,
And cherish the gift of who you are.

The Hands of Work

The hands of work are rough yet kind,
They shape the world, they forge, they bind.
They carve, they craft, they mend, they make,
They bear the weight that others take.
With every tool, with every nail,
They tell a story, rich and frail.
The hands of work, though tired and worn,
Hold dreams that rise with each new morn.
For in their grasp, creation lies,
A labour of love beneath the skies.

The Joy of Craft

In work, there's joy, a simple peace,
A flow where all distractions cease.
To shape, to build, to see things grow,
To feel the pride in what we know.
Each task completed, each goal attained,
A quiet triumph, a purpose gained.
The joy of craft, the heart's reward,
A moment where our dreams are stored.
Through work, we find the soul's delight,
A steady flame that burns so bright.

A Day's Work

A day's work done, the sun sinks low,
Its golden light begins to glow.
The tools are laid, the sweat wiped clean,
The quiet comes, a moment serene.
The heart feels full, the mind at rest,
For effort given brings life its zest.
Each hour spent, each job complete,
A steady rhythm, a life replete.
For in the work, we find our way,
And earn the peace at the end of the day.

The Builder's Legacy

Work is a legacy, built with care,
A lasting mark beyond compare.
The mason's wall, the writer's pen,
The sweat of hands, the dreams of men.
Each act of toil, each labor shared,
A world created, bold and dared.
Though years may pass, though time may fade,
The work endures, its foundation laid.
For every stone and word and deed,
Plants seeds of hope the future will need.

Through Struggles and Strides

Work is not easy, nor meant to be,
It teaches strength and humility.
Through struggles fierce, through uphill climbs,
We learn to weather life's tough times.
Each stride we make, each challenge met,
Builds a story we won't forget.
For in the effort, we find our core,
And open life's most hidden door.
Work shapes the soul, refines the heart,
And shows us all we can impart.

Work's Reward

The reward of work is more than gold,
It's in the stories that are told.
It's in the pride of a job well done,
In battles fought and victories won.
It's in the friendships forged through toil,
The satisfaction of the soil.
It's in the growth, the lessons learned,
The respect through labor rightly earned.
Work's true reward is the life we weave,
The legacy we choose to leave.

Work's Quiet Grace

Work carries a grace, silent and strong,
A quiet rhythm that hums along.
It lifts the weary, shapes the land,
It builds the world with steady hands.
No glory sought, no fame required,
Just hearts devoted, minds inspired.
Through every trade, through every chore,
Work gives us something to adore.
For in its quiet, humble way,
Work honours life, come what may.

Purpose in the Toil

In work, we find a purpose clear,
A reason for the sweat and tears.
It's not just labor, not just strife,
It's building meaning into life.
Each nail we hammer, each stone we lay,
Is part of something vast and grey.
Though weary hands may tremble, sore,
They hold the key to something more.
For in the toil, the truth is found:
Purpose gives life its solid ground.

About the Author

Darryl De Carteret Pochin spent much of his career serving in the demanding field of emergency services, where quick thinking and resilience were part of daily life. Throughout those intense years, writing remained a quiet but constant passion a creative outlet that allowed him to explore the power of storytelling. Now, with more time on his hands, Darryl is fully embracing his journey as a budding author.

Focusing on fictional stories, short stories, and poetry, Darryl channels his rich life experiences and keen observations into his writing. Whether crafting compelling narratives or thought-provoking poems, his work reflects a deep appreciation for human nature, emotions, and the small moments that shape our lives. His goal is simple: to keep improving as a writer and share stories that resonate with readers.

With a fresh perspective and a genuine love for the craft, Darryl Martel, is excited to continue growing as an author, honing his skills, and connecting with a wider audience.